MYTHS WE BELIEVE,

PREDATORS

37 THINGS YOU DON'T WANT TO
KNOW ABOUT ABUSE IN CHURCH
(BUT YOU REALLY SHOULD)

Also by Sarah McDugal

One Face: Shed the Mask, Own Your Values, and Lead Wisely

Safe Churches: Responding to Abuse in the Faith Community

MYTHS WE BELIEVE,

PREDATORS

37 THINGS YOU DON'T WANT TO
KNOW ABOUT ABUSE IN CHURCH
(BUT YOU REALLY SHOULD)

BY SARAH MCDUGAL
& DARON PRATT

MYTHS WE BELIEVE, PREDATORS WE TRUST...
37 THINGS YOU DON'T WANT TO KNOW ABOUT ABUSE IN CHURCH (BUT YOU REALLY SHOULD)

©2019 Sarah McDugal and Daron Pratt

Published by Wilder Journey Press.

www.WildernessToWILD.com
www.sarahmcdugal.com
Facebook: @SarahMcDugalAuthor

WILDER JOURNEY
PRESS

ISBN: 978-1-7334834-0-7

ASIN: B07VSKHS2R

Cover and Interior Design by:
Emmalee Shallenberger
Emmalee Designs
www.EmmaleeDesignsArt.com
Facebook: @EmmaleeDesignsArt

To the silenced ones.

From the Authors

As advocates against abuse in the faith community, we encounter many deeply rooted myths about abuse, sex offenders, and domestic violence. We find that scripture is commonly twisted to enable abusive behavior patterns at home and in church. Our hearts ache at the anguish caused by the misuse of God's words, and we grieve the ways God's character of love and protection is so often misrepresented.

Myths We Believe, Predators We Trust is our effort to shed light on just a few of these myths. Using expert knowledge, bible references, and proven research — we hope this little book will equip you to make your church safer.

Warmly,

Sarah & Daron

YOU'VE PROBABLY HEARD
A FEW OF THESE MYTHS,
AND YOU MAY EVEN
BELIEVE SOME OF
THEM.
WE DID TOO,
BEFORE WE
LEARNED
THE TRUTH
ABOUT
ABUSE.

Handling abuse in ways that are biblically redemptive yet legally sound is absolutely vital to the success of evangelism and retention in the faith community.

We become collaborators in abuse when we:

- ignore those who are being exploited or abused,

- prioritize the protection of abusers higher than their accountability for sin, or

- ignore or dismiss the need to extend safety and support to victims.

Sheep do not pretend to be wolves. Sheep do not act in patterns of evil and then cry crocodile tears to convince an audience that their repentance exists. If someone is acting like a wolf, it is not because they are a misguided sheep, it is because they are showing their true character. Shepherds who refuse to protect the sheep prove themselves to be hirelings, or worse, prove themselves to be wolves. Either way, the result is to destroy the flock.

Overlooking abuse misrepresents the character of God to those who have been harmed, as well as those who have watched the abuse second-hand, and turns them away from the heart of God.

Proverbs 31:8-9, Jeremiah 22:3

PERPETRATORS IN

CHURCH TEND TO BE

POPULAR AND POWERFUL.

We catch very few of the perpetrators in church. The worst are still moving freely in church. Clever perpetrators pass background checks, cheerfully complete safety trainings, and charmingly navigate the church system.

Programs that check backgrounds for church staff or volunteers are a helpful first step, but won't catch the most dangerous abusers. Most abusers aren't registered sex offenders, and won't be flagged by background checks. These individuals become actively involved in children's programs, serve in powerful church offices, and volunteer in positions of power where they can groom, test, and ultimately harm.

JimmyHinton.org

ABUSERS ARE EASY TO SPOT, SOCIALLY AWKWARD AND TEND TO STAY ON THE FRINGES.

Abusers intentionally cultivate trust in the community. Grooming means building trust not only with the target victim, but also with the entire church and even the surrounding community.

They test boundaries to determine who will allow liberties without reporting. This trust means you will believe their claims of innocence if they ever happen to be accused. This mode of operation allows access to abuse, and often guarantees getting away with it!

Perpetrators especially like to curry favor and build social equity with people in higher positions of power, in order to later provide cover and help silence victims who may try to speak out. When we blindly defend those accused of abuse, we fulfill exactly the role they have groomed us to play.

Abusers are your best friends, colleagues, leaders, or peers. An abuser will often work their way into positions of trust, leadership, or authority over many years before ever getting caught or even triggering suspicion. Their roles may range from organizational leadership (a source of prestige) to the janitor (a source of access and invisibility, which is a different type of power).

Perpetrators tend to be charming, approachable, friendly, helpful, and apparently indispensable — whatever will help to ensure your enthusiastic support and defense of their character. They purposefully cultivate your loyalty and support.

Predators by Anna C. Salter

Why Does He Do That? by Lundy Bancroft

Abusers are absolutely in church. Every church.

Perpetrators tend to choose vulnerable groups, situations, churches, victims — which allows them to control the narrative, perpetrate abuse, manipulate the evidence, blame the victim, and usually get away with it.

Abusers are masters at honing in on weaknesses that allow them to exploit places and people.

The more closed a community is — the more a culture tends toward authoritarian mindset (giving one gender power over the other, or placing unchecked influence in the hands of spiritual leaders), the more a congregation equates forgiveness with trust — the greater the risk of abuse taking place and being covered up.

How He Gets In Her Head by Don Hennessy

Flying Free with Natalie Anne Hoffman

THE BIGGEST MYTH: VICTIMS TELL LIES TO ACCUSE PERPETRATORS. THEY GENERALLY DON'T.

When the story breaks, you won't want to believe it. Your first reaction will likely be to think the victim must have made it up, is confused, or is telling lies. You might assume the alleged abuser must have surely been encouraged or invited by the victim in some way.

You will be drawn to support the perpetrator and rescue their reputation. You may instinctively condemn the victim and feel suspicious because they seem emotionally confused, difficult, or broken.

We see it happen again and again:
Highly educated people in positions of power will go to great lengths to defend the perpetrator. Everyone wants very badly to believe and support the perpetrator who has helped so many, done so much good, and generally appears to be beyond reproach.

Is It Me? by Natalie Anne Hoffman

Statistics show that 95 to 98% of abuse reports are true. It is vitally important to sort false claims from true ones, to avoid reputational assault. False allegations typically stem from some form of revenge or mental imbalance that can be discovered through careful investigation.

However, each report should also be viewed through the understanding that allegations are statistically more often true than untrue.

All abuse reports should be taken seriously and reported to the proper authorities. Every report should receive a thorough evaluation, professional investigation and compassionate response.

RAINN.org

False accusations are not the greatest risk to boys and men. In reality, males have a significantly greater risk of being sexually assaulted than of being falsely accused of assault.

One in 7 males are the victims of abuse. Fewer than 5% of abuse allegations are false. That means males are far more likely to be assaulted or abused, than to be blamed unjustly. Protecting our children, our churches, and our communities means protecting our boys from abuse as well as our girls.

Neither gender is less deserving of protection and justice.

RAINN.org

MYTH 9 | ABUSERS DON'T USUALLY HAVE MULTIPLE VICTIMS.

There is rarely ever just one victim. In reality, the average predator has 50 to 150 victims before their first arrest, and many more after arrest.

Rarely does an initial arrest lead to charges or prosecution. Fewer than six out of every 1,000 rapists ever spend a single day in jail.

Predators nearly always have multiple victims, and will often have several victims at the same time, in various grooming stages or degrees of abuse.

Predators by Anna C. Salter

WHEN SOMEONE IS ABUSED, THEY USUALLY TELL RIGHT AWAY.

Most victims never report. In contrast with popular assumptions, most victims do not come forward. The average age for those who disclose their child sexual abuse is 22 years after the final instance of abuse.

Why? Because victims are often threatened by the perpetrator with harm or exposure. Or if they did attempt to tell, they may have been urged by family and friends to get over it. If a relative or older sibling knew about a child's abuse, they may have dismissed it as "kiddie play" or refused to believe them because of the shame it would bring to the family. Sometimes, victims never realized the abuse was wrong until years later.

In many cases, it takes a female from 7-14 years to report abuse, while males may take closer to 20 years, if they ever do.

National Association for People Abused in Childhood

CHURCHES LOVE CHARMERS, AND WE HATE MESS.

MYTH 11 | IF SOMETHING WAS HAPPENING IN MY CHURCH, I'D BE ABLE TO TELL.

Perpetrators are skilled deceivers. If something appears strange or seems off, there is usually much more going on beneath the surface.

We'd all like to think that we can tell when someone has a propensity to do great evil. Studies show over and over again that we simply can't.

One in every 25 people in today's society is a sociopath — a person who completely lacks moral conscience. Just because someone has been kind and charming to you, doesn't mean they aren't capable of great evil toward someone else. It's unlikely that your radar (or prey-dar as we like to call it) is going to sense every person who lacks a conscience.

However, when you DO sense something is not right, don't ignore your instincts. Encourage your children to do the same — if something or someone makes them uncomfortable, teach them to go tell a trusted adult and keep telling until someone believes them.

The Sociopath Next Door by Dr. Martha Stout

Gift of Fear by Gavin de Becker

MYTH 12 | IF SOMEONE SAID THEY WERE BEING ABUSED, MY CHURCH WOULD DEFINITELY BELIEVE THEM.

Churches generally don't believe abuse reports. Abuse is messy. And complicated. It's far simpler to believe a victim invented or exaggerated allegations than to accept that someone you love, trust, respect, and admire is a perpetrator.

Don't assume that because someone is nice to you, they can't abuse someone else. Eagles may not attack their equals, but that doesn't mean they won't gobble up a mouse.

Believing the truth about abuse often means shattering everyone's sense of safety. After all, if this well-respected person could be living a double life, then who else might be secretly evil, too? Whom can you trust?

The most common reaction to suspected abuse is to turn a blind eye or convince ourselves it is none of our business. Perpetrators know this and they use it to access more victims.

Predators by Anna C. Salter

Many churches protect perpetrators instead of the victim. The perpetrator usually presents well and appears more believable.

Their story is convincingly delivered, and appears to make sense. Churches often assume forgiveness should be followed by rapid reinstatement to influential positions, which means the perpetrator can abuse again and again.

Church leaders tend to roll out a red carpet of belief, love, forgiveness, support, restoration, and even promotion. Often, congregations resist putting any form of safety agreement in place or enforcing its conditions.

Even when perpetrators are registered sex offenders or convicted criminals, they typically are still allowed to interact with the church freely, under the guise of forgiveness.

This misplaced protection is a significant factor in how churches enable abusers to accumulate multiple victims.

JimmyHinton.org

A PERSON WHO KEEPS MAKING NOISE
ABOUT ABUSE ISSUES IS A TROUBLEMAKER.

Often those who report abuse are persecuted and pushed out.
We don't like uncomfortable stories unless they come from far away and
already have a happy ending.

Someone trying to heal from trauma may appear difficult or act out in
bizarre or confrontational ways. They may be labeled the "naughty child"
or the "rebel". What they actually need is support, protection, provision,
and healing. This requires the church to come alongside them, get
involved in the mess, and do the hard work of sorting out the truth and
finding solutions.

The perpetrator asks only that everyone return to normal; maintain
the status quo; smile, nod, and do life as usual. The perpetrator makes
solutions feel simple and easy in comparison. It's no surprise churches
may breathe a sigh of relief if the victim disappears.

Most victims just silently leave. Unresolved trauma creates barriers in healing, leading many continue to suffer in silence. It is generally easier for victims to walk away than to face the perpetrator, their enablers, and the collective misrepresentation of God's character over and over again.

Victims may find it easier to fade away and silently vanish, than to face the ongoing environment of diminishing, disbelief, and dismissal that is common in churches.

Give Her Wings

FEWER THAN 1 IN 10

ABUSERS WILL DO

WHAT IT TAKES TO

GENUINELY CHANGE.

SEXUAL ADDICTION AND ABUSE IS AN ADULT ISSUE.

Predators often begin abusing when they are young.
The average age of exposure to hardcore pornography is currently around eight years old.

As children's perception of sexuality is increasingly shaped around the exploitation, violence, and dehumanization of women showcased in pornography, they are more and more likely to act out the pornographic content they have viewed as they interact with their peers.

Peer-on-peer abuse is commonly overlooked and easily hidden. Sexual addiction often begins early, especially as children are exposed to pornography at younger and younger ages.

Seducers Among Our Children by Patrick Crough

WHEN AN ABUSER CRIES AND SAYS THEY'VE CHANGED, WE SHOULD BELIEVE THEM AND EXTEND GRACE.

There is no scientific evidence, as yet, that a sexual abuser will change. While God is absolutely capable of bringing healing and transforming a repentant abuser; it is rare for an abuser to choose to submit to a thorough process of change. Instead, it is common to feign repentance just long enough to regain trust and discredit their victims, before moving on to abuse again.

The only solution is for the faith community to hold perpetrators accountable by insisting on tangible proof of long-term change, as well as providing educated risk assessments and safety agreements.

God shows grace and forgiveness, but actions still bring consequences we cannot and should not overlook.

Predators by Anna C. Salter, Why Does He Do That? by Lundy Bancroft

MYTH 18 | IF AN ABUSER HAS ACTED REPENTANT FOR AT LEAST SIX MONTHS, WE SHOULD TRUST THEM AGAIN.

Long-term accountability needs to last longer than you think.
By definition, abusers already live double lives and are capable of overwhelming levels of deceit. This factor must be considered in any assessments of genuine repentance.

Abuse recovery experts state that an abuser needs to participate in professional therapy three to four times per week, for at least four to five years, before authentic change can be assessed.

Comparatively short stints of persuasive confessions, good behavior, rehabilitation, therapy, or other interventions will not result in lasting change and cannot be the basis of restored trust or reinstatement.

Mad About Marriage with Mike Tucker

Psalm 82 Initiative

MYTH 19 | COURTS OFTEN GET IT WRONG AND CHURCHES SHOULD BE KNOWN FOR GRACE, FORGIVENESS, AND SECOND CHANCES.

If someone is convicted in a court of law, churches cannot ignore the evidence. If a convicted offender seeks to come to church, begs to avoid accountability or other safety structures, or fails to disclose relevant history — the church must take action.

Only 1% of reported cases actually make it to court. This does not mean 99% of reported cases are false, just that the system is overloaded.

At no time is it acceptable to overlook a conviction based on the abuser's persuasive story or tears.

RAINN.org

FAITH COMMUNITIES TYPICALLY TEND TO MISUNDERSTAND, MISDIAGNOSE, AND MISHANDLE ABUSE.

IF SOMEONE WAS NEVER CONVICTED IN A CRIMINAL COURT, WE SHOULD ASSUME THEY'RE INNOCENT.

Absence of criminal conviction does not equal innocence. If the perpetrator is not convicted, people typically assume he was innocent.

This naïveté fails to account for the many reasons a guilty person may avoid conviction — plea bargains, overloaded court dockets, evidentiary technicalities, or the discretion of a district attorney... all may result in the perpetrator walking free.

Churches are responsible to uphold a standard of both moral decency and civil safety. The faith community does not need to wait to take action until a case meets the criminal evidentiary standard of "beyond reasonable doubt".

If an abuse report is more likely true than untrue, churches must take protective action to ensure the integrity of the organization and the safety of the vulnerable.

Ephesians 5:3-6

Matthew 18 was never intended for resolving abuse. Church leaders often point to Matthew 18:15-17 as a conflict-resolution formula between abuser and victim. It's actually a format for helping a peer stop doing something that hurt you, or is hurting themselves. The wording "if a brother sins" implies equality between you and the other person — not the power imbalance that is created between abuser and victim.

Clergy may misquote Scripture by saying "Go speak privately to the person who harmed you, before you come for pastoral counseling." Or, "That didn't work? Go back again, and take a neutral friend along." This strategy is unbiblical in situations of abuse, and those who promote this solution cause harm to both victim and abuser.

That doesn't mean Jesus wants us to avoid dealing with abuse. He addressed abuse earlier in verses 5-6, saying that anyone who hurts "a little one" should have a millstone tied around their neck and be thrown into the sea. In this context, the words used for "little ones" mean anyone with lesser power or ability. That means it can refer to children, the elderly, or those who are vulnerable in other ways.

God has strong feelings about holding abusers accountable. But the Divine approach to resolution places the burden of change on the abuser, not the victim.

Matthew 18:5-6, Matthew 18:15-17, Mark 9:42

SCRIPTURE TEACHES US TO HANDLE ABUSE INTERNALLY.

No, Scripture teaches that abusers should have severe consequences.
In the Old Testament, when Israel was ruled by a theocracy (governed by God, rather than by a human king), the civil justice system and the church community were intertwined.

Moses' laws defined severe consequences for sexual assault, exploitation, and abuse. Under Mosaic law, there were no rapists or adulterers left alive to move freely in the community or interact with victims during seasons of rehabilitation — because Israel had a strict justice system that punished assault and sexual sin by death.

Today's civil and criminal systems function outside the faith community, but that does not mean abuse should be left unaddressed. Handling abuse internally leads to disaster, and is against the law.

Churches must become willing to take active steps to get help, report to police, bring in a consultant* specializing in situational abuse resolution, and otherwise focus on God's core principle of protecting the vulnerable.

Deuteronomy 22:25-27, Romans 13:1-5

*See RECOMMENDATIONS for consultants.

Church members are typically reticent to report. Church members often hesitate to report suspicions of abuse due to the myth that "good believers" cannot take a fellow church member to court. Other reasons people fail to report include self-doubt, uncertainty, relationship with the abuser, and the assumption that it is none of our business.

Every state has mandatory reporting laws, and individuals who work with children are generally required to report any suspicion of abuse. Moreover, believers are mandated by Scripture to protect the vulnerable.

This means it is absolutely vital to report any suspected abuse or inappropriate activity with a minor. Once a report has been made, it is also crucial to provide compassionate, ongoing support to the minor and their family.

1 Peter 2:13-14, Romans 13:3-4

Church leaders who enable abusers are misrepresenting God's character. Too often, the faith community assumes that a legal conviction, the loss of employment, public embarrassment, or other peripheral consequences should be considered punishment enough.

We find it easier to wish reconciliation into existence than to stay involved in the process of safety monitoring and risk the wrath of an unrepentant predator who insists on their "rights" to maintain access to power and influence.

When the faith community doesn't insist on appropriate ongoing accountability structures, require abusers to cooperate with long-term therapy, and implement appropriate safety structures — we are refusing to prioritize the protection of future victims. In doing so, we also misrepresent God's character of love and justice on behalf of his wounded little ones.

Psalm 94:23, 1 Thessalonians 1:9

OUR THEOLOGY INFLUENCES HOW WE RESPOND TO BOTH PERPETRATORS AND VICTIMS.

MYTH 25 | WHEN YOU FORGIVE SOMETHING, YOU AREN'T SUPPOSED TO BRING IT UP EVER AGAIN.

Warped theologies trap victims into unbiblical demands. When God talks about forgiving sins and burying them in the depths of the sea, we tend to overlook the phrase that says He tramples the sins first. Active, ongoing sin is not trampled yet and won't be cast into the sea.

When we confuse forgiveness with trustful reconciliation, rather than focusing on the necessary accountability for the abuser's actions, we damage the path to salvation for both victim and abuser. Restoration must only follow proven transformation; restoration cannot not precede repentance.

Forgiveness supplied is the forgiveness we hold in our hearts for the unrepentant person. Jesus said, "Whenever you stand praying, if you have anything against anyone, forgive him, that your Father in heaven may also forgive your trespasses" (Mark 11:25).

Forgiveness applied is forgiveness bestowed upon someone who is truly, deeply repentant. Jesus said, "If your brother sins against you, rebuke him; and if he repents, forgive him" (Luke 17:3). Notice that forgiveness is "if" he repents. The forgiveness we hold in store for our abusers can only be applied if they truly repent.

Micah 7:19

Black and White Bible, Black and Blue Wife by Ruth A Tucker

Pressuring victims to reconcile, to forgive, even to leave before they are ready — is abuse in its own right. The greatest need of an abuse victim is to rediscover their own voice and their own individual identity as God created them to be.

Telling victims that they must heal faster, forgive sooner, or reconcile with their abuser means you are taking away their right to free choice. That is exactly what their abuser already did.

When we realize someone in danger, it is easy to want to rescue them. If the victim isn't convinced that it's time to leave, helpers often feel their efforts were useless. But again, you cannot force someone to leave if they aren't ready. Forcing someone to receive help, even with the "best of intentions," is to treat them as incompetent, taking on the role of abuser while trying to help.

Jeremiah 22:3, Psalm 103:6

Healing from Hidden Abuse by Shannon Thomas

The best way to love an abuser well is to insist on consequences. It's tempting to want to let things go, hope for the best, and seek to return to the status quo. It's tempting to leave out details "to protect the community."

Resist those temptations!

The goal for any abusive situation is to do what is most likely to bring salvation to both victim and abuser. That means insisting on consequences for sin that are strong enough to create the impetus for lasting change, rather than empowering the abuser to continue to lie, manipulate, and self-deceive.

Jude 1:22-23, Isaiah 26:10

Pornography is biblical adultery. Jesus Christ stated unequivocally that to look at a woman with lust is to commit adultery in the mind. This means any pursuit of lustful arousal by anyone other than your spouse — whether on a screen, with a magazine, in person, or using other erotic literature — meets the New Testament definition of adultery.

Pornography is also a form of sexual abuse. Addiction to pornography is now known to be a contributing factor in reduced capacity for intimacy, increased aggression and sexual violence, increased rates of depression and erectile dysfunction, and other forms of domestic abuse.

Abuse recovery advocates have observed pornography to be a consistently present factor in case after case of domestic and spiritual abuse in the faith community.

Job 31:1,11, Matthew 5:28-29, Colossians 3:5,
Betrayal Trauma Recovery

Our theology conditions us to believe that accusers are lying.
Scripture often refers to Satan as "the Accuser," and we all know Satan is a liar who falsely accuses God. The entire Judeo-Christian theology of good and evil is rooted in the defense of God's character against false onslaughts from the Accuser.

Throughout the biblical narrative, we teach that the Accuser is out to lie, cheat, steal, and destroy. His accusations are rooted in things like pride, jealousy, revenge, and lust for fame.

Consequently, when believers hear of a victim making "accusations" against someone who is respected, trusted, admired, and loved by the community — it's no great leap to assume that any human accuser is driven by similar motivations. It's almost instinctive to leap to the defense of the accused, just like we've been taught that it's our job to defend the goodness of God.

When we fall into this trap, we unwittingly misrepresent the character of God toward the vulnerable, the oppressed, the innocent, and the wounded.

Proverbs 31:8-9

DO YOU KNOW SIGNS

WHEN AN ADULT MAY

BE EXPLOITING THEIR

RELATIONSHIP WITH A CHILD

FOR SEXUAL REASONS?

It may not be obvious when an adult is using their relationship with a child for sexual reasons. We may feel vaguely uncomfortable about the way they play with the child, or favor them, or create reasons to be alone with little ones. Be aware of the signs of possible child abuse.

This is not a comprehensive list, but there may be cause for concern about an adult or young person if they:

- Refuse to allow a child sufficient privacy or to make their own decisions on personal matters.

- Insist on physical affection such as kissing, hugging or wrestling even when the child clearly does not want it.

- Are overly interested in the sexual development of a child or teenager.

- Insist on time alone with a child with no interruptions.

- Spend most of their spare time with children and have little interest in spending time with people their own age.

- Regularly offer to babysit children for free or take children on overnight outings alone.

- Buy children expensive gifts or give them money for no apparent reason.

- Walk in on children or teenagers in the bathroom.

- Treat a particular child as a favorite, making them feel 'special' compared with others.

- Pick on a particular child.

Parents Protect

There are three types of child abusers, but only one type is sexually attracted to children. We often assume all people who hurt children are pedophiles. They're not. The perpetrator's friends or supporters may decry the allegation of abuse, saying, "How dare you call him a pedophile!?"

In reality, a child abuser may not be a pedophile at all.

Pedophiles — are physically attracted to and aroused by underage children. In reality, many pedophiles may never touch or harm a child in their entire lives. Being sexually attracted to children is not a guarantee that a person will take action in real life to harm a child. (This doesn't make pedophilia morally acceptable, of course.)

Child Predators — are those who invest time, attention, and calculated energy into testing, grooming, and cultivating trust with children, parents, surrounding leaders, and the rest of the community. These are quite often heterosexual males who are attracted to adult female partners and may be married and have their own children. Predators aren't sexually attracted to children, but they love the power of control. They get off on the game of it. These are the hardest to detect, the most convincing charmers, the least often caught, and by far the most dangerous.

Child Molesters — are anyone who has sexually abused a child for any reason. These may lack the cunning of the predator, and are not pedophiles. They harm children out of impulse, convenience, or as a means to another end, such as obtaining drugs or getting ahead. Children are collateral damage in their quest for self-gratification.

Dr. David Finkelhor, Crimes Against Children Research Center,

University of New Hampshire

Predators do not abuse children out of a need for sex. Abuse is about power and control — not sex. Most child abusers are heterosexual and are often married. These predators do not abuse due to a spouse withholding sex in the marriage.

Child abuse isn't about sex.

Most child abuse cases involve a trusted friend or family relationship between the minor victim and the offender. Fifteen percent of abusers are the victim's biological father. The rest tend to be boyfriends, stepfathers, or other adult males in an authority role.

Predators by Anna C. Salter,

Why Does He Do That? by Lundy Bancroft

MYTH 7: SOMETIMES CHILDREN LEAD ABUSERS ON AND ASK FOR IT.

Children cannot entice abuse. Period. A minor is below the age of consent and legally is without responsibility for any form of abuse.

Children cannot be blamed for, or assumed to have encouraged their own abuse. The differential in power of an adult over a child removes the option of projecting blame on the child.

No child should be considered complicit in their own abuse in any way.

Predators by Anna C. Salter

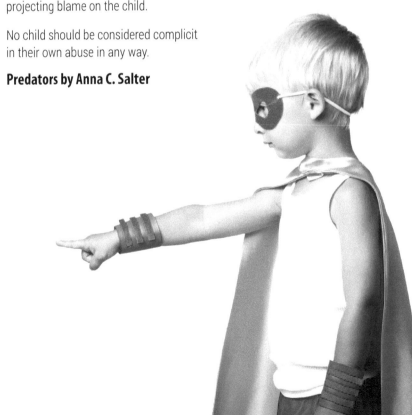

Your children are less likely to tell you than you think they are.
Educate and equip your children with knowledge and practical tools*
about safe and unsafe touch. Talk to them openly from a young age
about the risks of pornography, what addiction does to your brain, and
what to do if someone exposes them to pornographic material.

Explain to kids that secrets are unhealthy and unsafe. Surprises are
things that will make someone happy and you keep it to yourself for
just a little while until it's time to tell. Secrets are things that will make
someone sad, get someone in trouble, or make someone afraid, and
the other person says you're never supposed to tell. If anyone (child or
grownup) tells you to keep a secret, you must tell a trusted parent or
adult right away!

Remind them that they can always talk to you as a parent, without
getting in trouble for what someone else did to them, no matter what
happens. If someone does something that makes them uncomfortable,
it is not their fault — it is the fault of the person who chose to do wrong.

*See RECOMMENDATIONS for parent resources.

**ALL POWER GIVEN
BY GOD IS INTENDED
TO PROTECT, NEVER
TO EXPLOIT.**

MYTH 35 | ABUSE IS CAUSED BY ANGER PROBLEMS OR CHILDHOOD TRAUMA AND WE SHOULD FEEL SORRY FOR ABUSERS.

All abuse is rooted in a sense of entitlement, power, and control.
God operates on the principle of free will. We can choose what path we wish to take, even though we are not free from the consequences of our choices.

When it comes to abuse situations, our duty is to DO justice even while we LOVE mercy. Too often we invert these instructions and end up loving justice but doing mercy. In cases of abuse, the most merciful action is to do justice.

Our biblical calling is to serve with humility, do justly, and cultivate the fruits of the Spirit — love, joy, peace, patience, kindness, goodness, faithfulness, gentleness, self-control — regardless of our gender.

To act with coercion, manipulation, deception, possession, forcefulness, and any other form of taking power over another person, is to emulate the tactics of Lucifer rather than Christ.

Philippians 2:8-9

Galatians 5:22

Micah 6:8

We cannot assume the abuse was a one-time lapse instead of a predatory pattern. It is painful and disturbing to accept that someone we know may have cultivated a double life to the point they would be capable of great harm. Never assume that you know all the facts just because you are a leader, friend, or family member. Often, only the victim knows the full story.

Predators will insist their abuse is an anomaly, a one-time slip, an unexpected moral fall — and we are comforted to believe them because the alternative is too shocking and messy to accept. However, this is rarely true.

There is no such thing as a "moral fall" because we fall in the place where we are already standing. Someone who chooses to harm a vulnerable person has already rejected the Holy Spirit in their mind until hardness of heart has become a habit.

2 Timothy 3:1-2

We cannot guarantee church safety, but we can take steps to make it harder to harm and safer to report. Churches need to adhere to biblical counsel on protecting the vulnerable, as well as acting with legal responsibility.

To do so, we must comply with offender and probation limitations, follow advice by those trained in trauma and abuse, and cooperate with civil authorities.

1) Put in place strict codes of conduct.

2) Enforce thorough background checks.

3) Train all church leaders in recognizing abuse and responding to trauma.

4) Provide comprehensive education to parents and children.

5) Insist that all reports are referred to appropriate authorities.

6) Make safe reporting options consistently accessible.

7) Cultivate a culture of open communication on the topics of abuse, healing, and recovery.

Jeremiah 13:20-21, 25

Recommended Consulting/Training Organizations:

Sarah McDugal - Abuse Recovery Coach
sarahmcdugal.com/

Wilderness to WILD - Courses and Resources for Survivors of Abuse
wildernesstowild.com/

Brave Hearts - Australia's Leading Child Protection Organization
bravehearts.org.au/

*Recommended Books to Read on Your Path to Healing After Abuse
sarahmcdugal.com/best-books-to-read/

*Recommended Books for Parents to Teach Kids About Addiction, Pornography, and Sex in a Biblical Way
sarahmcdugal.com/sex/

*Children & Porn - *Printable PDF Download*
**cdn.disciple.org.au/wp-content/uploads/
2018/07/24094653/Children-and-Porn.pdf**

DEVELOPMENT

HERE I STAND,

FOR THE VICTIMS,

FOR OUR CHILDREN

AUTHORS

Sarah McDugal

is an Author, International Speaker, and Abuse Recovery Coach, based in the United States. She is a survivor and the mother of two children. Sarah coaches women in the faith community who are healing from abusive relationships. Her passion is to lead women out of the wilderness and into a wild, abundant life with Jesus.

Pastor Daron Pratt

is a Children, Family and Junior Youth Ministries Director in North New South Wales, Australia. He is married to Lisa, and they have two children. Daron is passionate about the importance of bringing churches and homes together with a strategic focus on raising children to love God.

Printed in the USA
CPSIA information can be obtained
at www.ICGtesting.com
LVHW061614280124
770153LV00005B/126